TUI

D1154920

SKJC

OCT -- 2017

GHOST
HOUSES

by Jessica Rudolph

Consultant: Ursula Bielski
Author and Paranormal Researcher
Founder of Chicago Hauntings, Inc.

BEARPORT
PUBLISHING

New York, New York

Credits

Cover, © Gulden Kunter Tikiroglu/iStock; TOC, © Eponaleah/Shutterstock and © Jagoush/Shutterstock; 4–5, © Razvan Ionut Dragomirescu/Shutterstock; 6, © kropic1/Shutterstock; 7, © Everett Historical/Shutterstock; 7T, © GL Archive/Alamy; 8, © FABIANO/SIPA/Newscom; 9, © Everett Historical/Shutterstock; 10, © Franck Fotos/Alamy; 11T, © ajt/Shutterstock; 11B, Public Domain; 12, Public Domain; 13, © FILE PHOTO KRT/Newscom; 14, © Gettysburg Tours; 15T, © The Miriam and Ira D. Wallach Division of Art, Prints and Photographs: Photography Collection, The New York Public Library; 15, © Niday Picture Library/Alamy; 16–17, © Merydolla/Shutterstock; 16, © Gettysburg Tours; 17, © Donna Beeler/Shutterstock; 18, © Sytilin Pavel/Shutterstock; 19, © Greg Vaughn/Alamy; 20, © MARGRIT HIRSCH/Shutterstock; 21, © Iriana Shiyan/Shutterstock; 21BR, © Duncan Walker; 23, © Stephanie Connell/Shutterstock.

Publisher: Kenn Goin
Editor: J. Clark
Creative Director: Spencer Brinker
Photo Researcher: Thomas Persano
Cover: Kim Jones

Library of Congress Cataloging-in-Publication Data

Names: Rudolph, Jessica, author.
Title: Ghost houses / by Jessica Rudolph.
Description: New York : Bearport Publishing Company, Inc., 2017. | Series: Tiptoe into scary places | Includes bibliographical references and index.
Identifiers: LCCN 2016038810 (print) | LCCN 2016039037 (ebook) | ISBN 9781684020454 (library) | ISBN 9781684020973 (ebook)
Subjects: LCSH: Haunted houses—Juvenile literature. | Ghosts—Juvenile literature.
Classification: LCC BF1475 .R83 2017 (print) | LCC BF1475 (ebook) | DDC 133.1/22—dc23
LC record available at https://lccn.loc.gov/2016038810

Copyright © 2017 Bearport Publishing Company, Inc. All rights reserved. No part of this publication may be reproduced in whole or in part, stored in any retrieval system, or transmitted in any form or by any means, electronic, mechanical, photocopying, recording, or otherwise, without written permission from the publisher.

For more information, write to Bearport Publishing Company, Inc., 45 West 21st Street, Suite 3B, New York, New York 10010. Printed in the United States of America.

10 9 8 7 6 5 4 3 2 1

CONTENTS

Ghost Houses

It's a cloudy night. Bats fly overhead as you walk past a dark, empty house. It looks like no one has lived there for years. Suddenly, you think you see a pair of eyes watching from the top window. Then the eyes vanish! Was it just your imagination?

Get ready to read four spooky tales about haunted houses. Turn the page . . . if you have the nerve!

"THE PRESIDENT WAS KILLED"

White House, Washington, DC

In 1865, President Abraham Lincoln had a terrible dream. In it, he saw a soldier guarding a **corpse** in the White House. When Lincoln asked who had died, the soldier said, "The President was killed by an **assassin**."

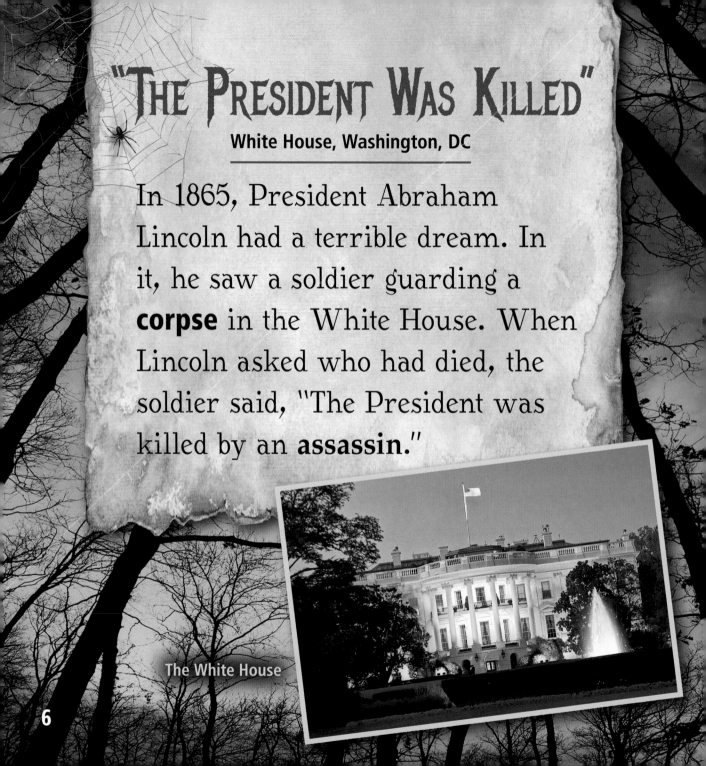

The White House

One month later, Lincoln was murdered.

Lincoln was watching a play in a theater when he was shot.

The gun that killed Lincoln

Since his death, many people have seen Lincoln's **spirit.** In the 1940s, a visitor spent the night at the White House. She was awakened by a knock on her door. When she opened it, there stood the ghost of Lincoln.

The Lincoln bedroom at the White House

8

The visitor fainted at the sight of the spirit! When she woke up, Lincoln's ghost was gone.

THE AX MURDERER

Many visitors to the Borden House see and hear strange things. Why? It might be because two people were **brutally** murdered there.

The Lizzie Borden House

10

One day in 1892, a woman named Abby Borden was making her bed. Suddenly, someone snuck up behind her. The person struck her with an ax. After 19 blows to the head, Abby was dead.

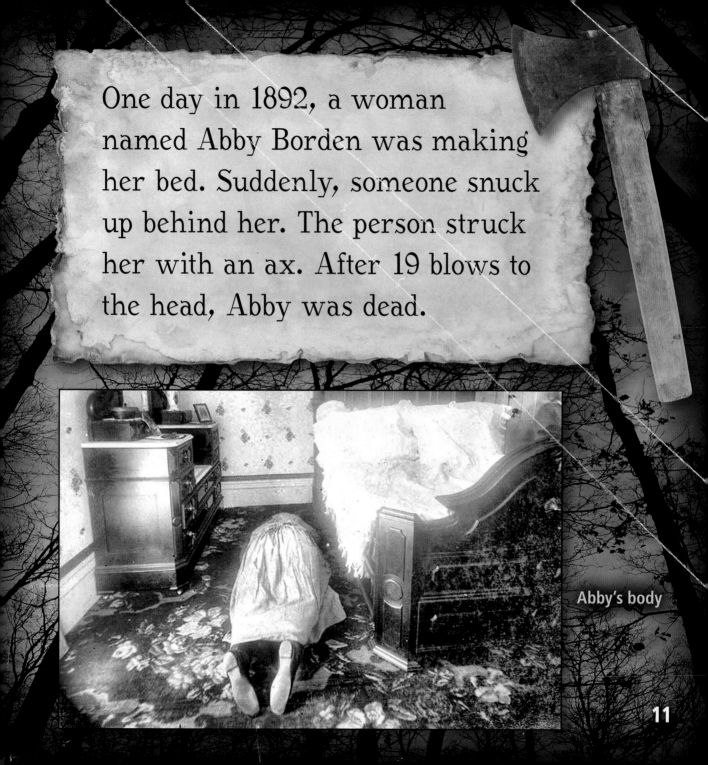

Abby's body

11

Moments later, the killer slipped into the living room. Abby's husband was taking a nap there. *Whack! Whack! Whack!* He was murdered in the same **gruesome** way.

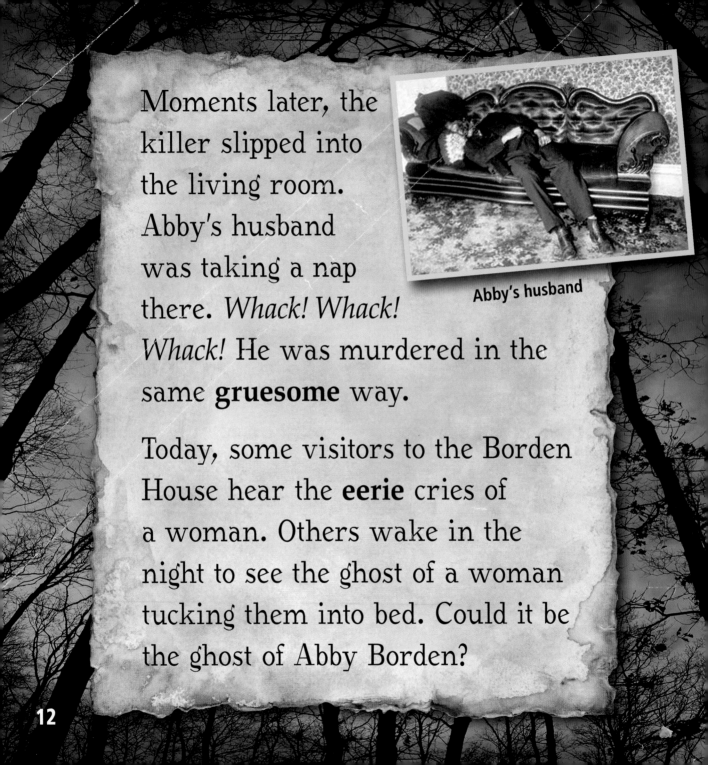

Abby's husband

Today, some visitors to the Borden House hear the **eerie** cries of a woman. Others wake in the night to see the ghost of a woman tucking them into bed. Could it be the ghost of Abby Borden?

The Borden's daughter, Lizzie, was put on **trial** for their murder. However, there wasn't enough **evidence** to prove she had killed her parents, so she was freed.

SHOT DURING BATTLE

Jennie Wade House, Gettysburg, Pennsylvania

There are many bullet holes on the outside of the Jennie Wade House. More than 150 years ago, the deadliest Civil War battle broke out in Gettysburg. Jennie and her family lived in a house right in the middle of the war zone.

Bullet holes

The Jennie Wade House

Jennie wanted to help the Northern soldiers, so she baked bread for them. It was dangerous work. *Pow! Pow! Pow!* Southern soldiers shot at the house day and night.

Jennie Wade

The American Civil War (1861–1865) was fought between the Northern and Southern states.

On July 3, 1863, just as Jennie was bending over the oven, a bullet tore through the front door. She was hit in the back. Jennie slumped over. Blood spilled on the floor. She was dead within minutes.

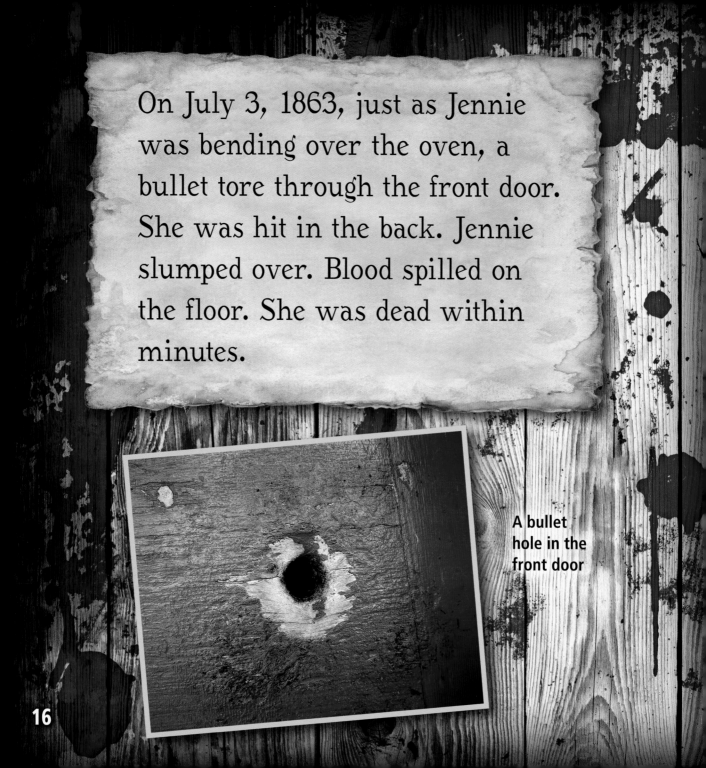

A bullet hole in the front door

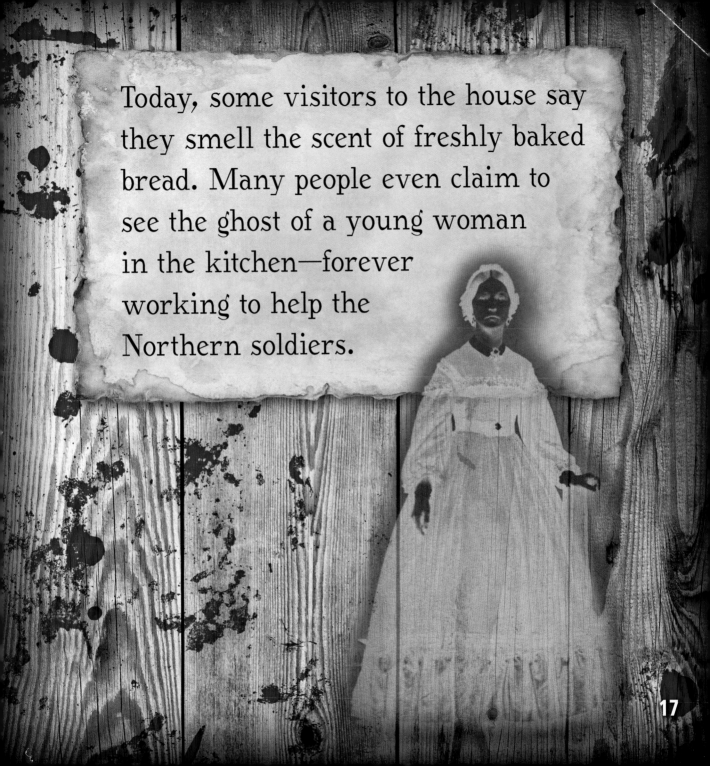

Today, some visitors to the house say they smell the scent of freshly baked bread. Many people even claim to see the ghost of a young woman in the kitchen—forever working to help the Northern soldiers.

THE MOST HAUNTED HOUSE?

Whaley House, San Diego, California

Why is the Whaley House known as one of the most haunted houses in America? It all started with a thief named "Yankee" Jim Robinson. In 1852, he was caught stealing a boat. He was hanged for his crime.

Five years later, Thomas Whaley and his wife, Anna, built a house on the spot where Yankee Jim was **executed**.

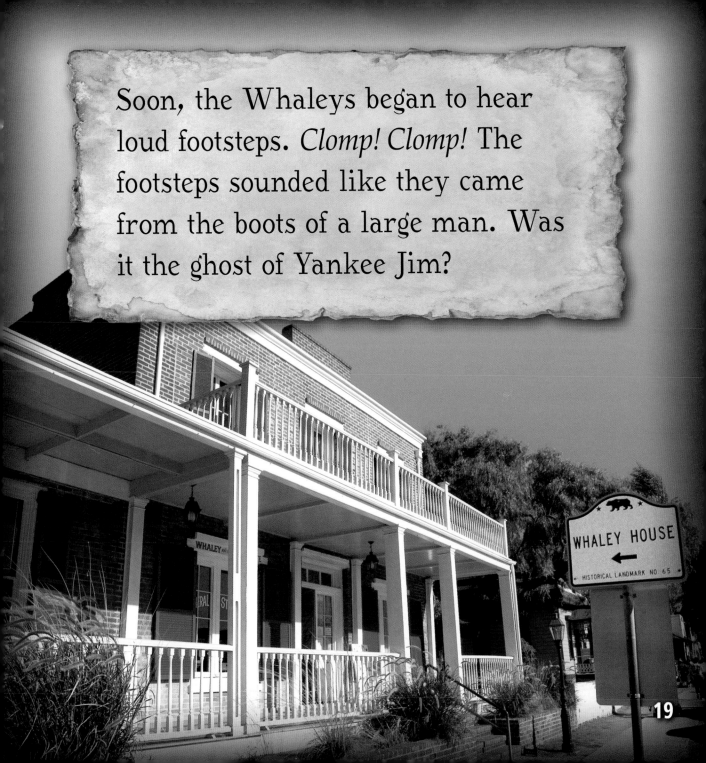

Soon, the Whaleys began to hear loud footsteps. *Clomp! Clomp!* The footsteps sounded like they came from the boots of a large man. Was it the ghost of Yankee Jim?

WHALEY HOUSE

HISTORICAL LANDMARK NO. 65

Then, terrible things began to happen in the house. The Whaley's baby son became sick and died. In 1885, their grown daughter shot and killed herself. Thomas and Anna were overcome with sadness. Had the ghost of Yankee Jim put a **curse** on the house?

Today, people who have visited the house say they have seen odd things. One little girl saw the spirit of Thomas . . . then he disappeared before her eyes. Thomas may be doomed to live in the house, forever **grieving** the loss of his children.

Visitors to the Whaley House have also reported feelings of being watched, seeing flickering lights, and experiencing **cold spots**.

GHOST HOUSES
IN AMERICA

WHALEY HOUSE
San Diego, California

Come see the site where a thief was hanged and a house was cursed.

JENNIE WADE HOUSE
Gettysburg, Pennsylvania

Visit a ghostly baker at a home filled with bullet holes.

LIZZIE BORDEN HOUSE
Fall River, Massachusetts

Check out the scene of two horrifying murders!

WHITE HOUSE
Washington, DC

Visit the famous home of a president's ghost.

Arctic Ocean

NORTH AMERICA

EUROPE

ASIA

Atlantic Ocean

Pacific Ocean

AFRICA

Pacific Ocean

SOUTH AMERICA

Indian Ocean

Atlantic Ocean

AUSTRALIA

Southern Ocean

ANTARCTICA

GLOSSARY

assassin (uh-SASS-in) a person who kills a famous person

brutally (BROO-tuhl-ee) very cruelly

cold spots (KOHLD SPAHTS) areas where the air feels colder than the air around it, thought by some to be caused by ghosts

corpse (KORPS) a dead body

curse (KURSS) a spell that brings unhappiness or bad luck

eerie (IHR-ee) mysterious, strange

evidence (EV-uh-duhnss) facts that prove that a crime has taken place

executed (EK-suh-*kyoo*-tid) put to death

grieving (GREEV-ing) feeling great sadness

gruesome (GROO-suhm) horrible and disgusting

sprit (SPIHR-it) a supernatural being, such as a ghost

trial (TRYE-uhl) an examination of facts in a court to decide if a charge is true

Index

Read More

Ketteman, Helen. *At the Old Haunted House.* New York: Two Lions (2014).

Speregen, Devra Newberger. *Curse of the Haunted House (Cold Whispers).* New York: Bearport (2016).

Learn More Online

To learn more about ghost houses, visit:
www.bearportpublishing.com/Tiptoe

About the Author

Jessica Rudolph is a writer and editor from Connecticut. She generally tries to avoid haunted houses, but hopes to bump into Lincoln's ghost while touring the White House one day.